MW00934740

Floral Mandala
Coloring Book

World's Most Beautiful Floral Mandalas
for Stress Relief and Relaxation

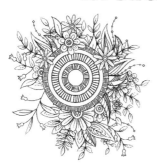 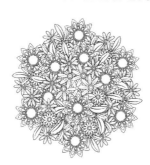 

Copyright 2018 © Coloring Book Cafe

All Rights Reserved.

PUBLISHED BY THE FRUITFUL MIND LTD.

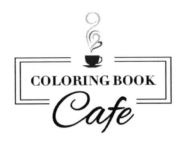

Disclaimer

All rights reserved. No part of this publication or the information in it may be quoted from or reproduced in any form by means such as printing, scanning, photocopying or otherwise without prior written permission of the copyright holder.

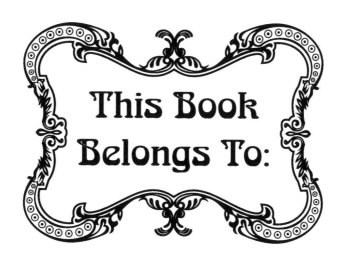

This Book
Belongs To:

BONUS

Relax And Create Your Own Masterpiece With
THIS 10 PAGE FREE *Beautiful Adult Coloring Book*

Claim Your FREE Coloring Book at:

www.freecoloringbooklet.com

Samples Below

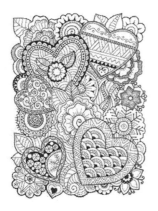 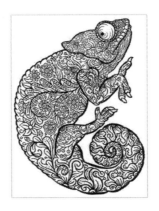 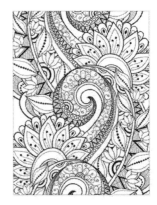

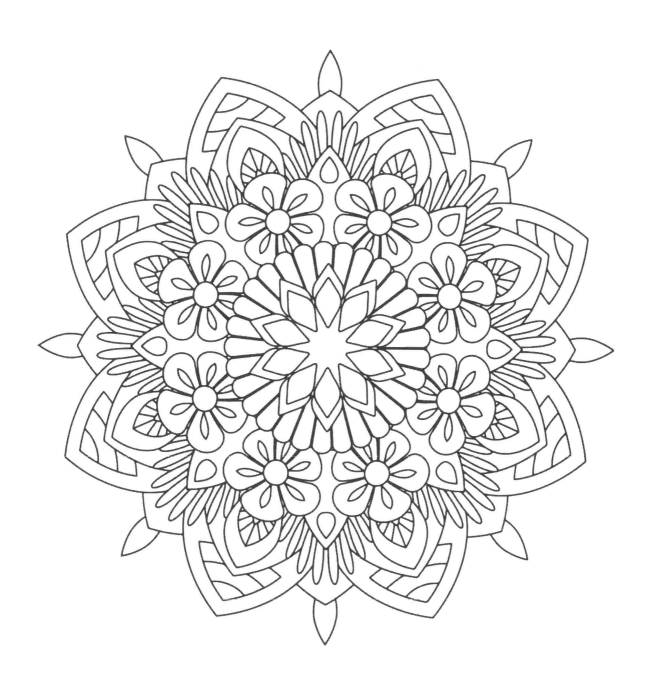

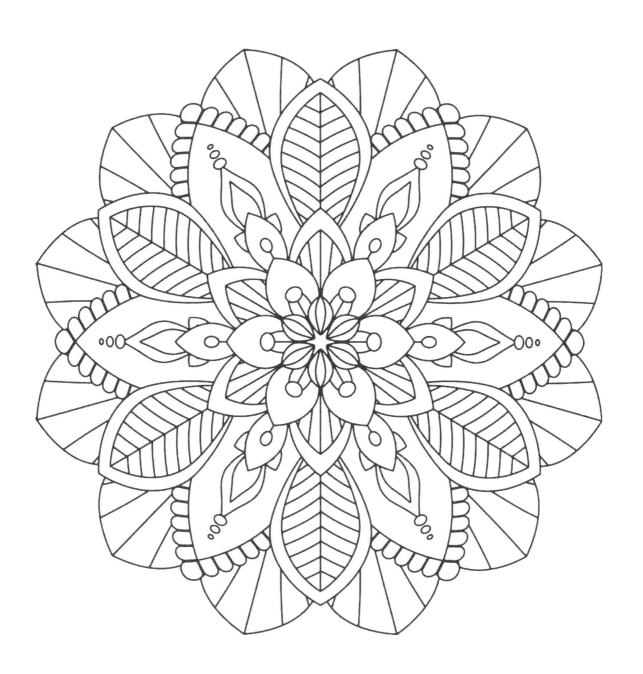

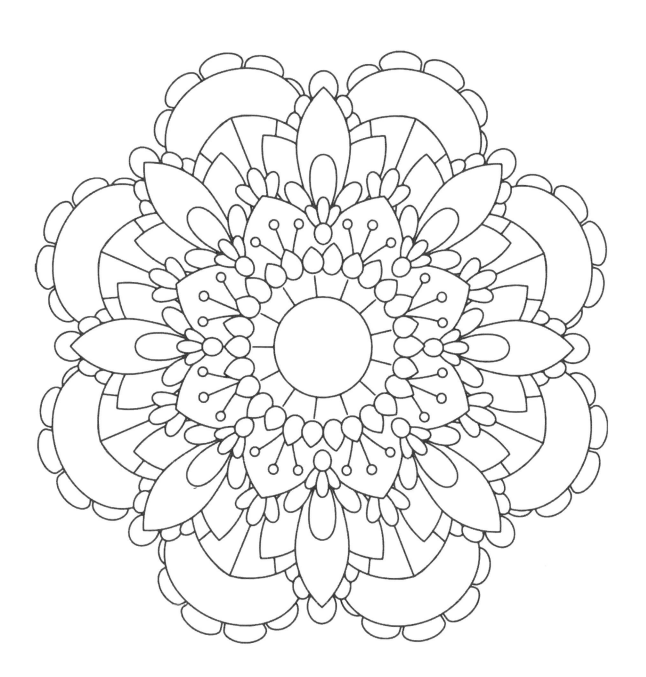

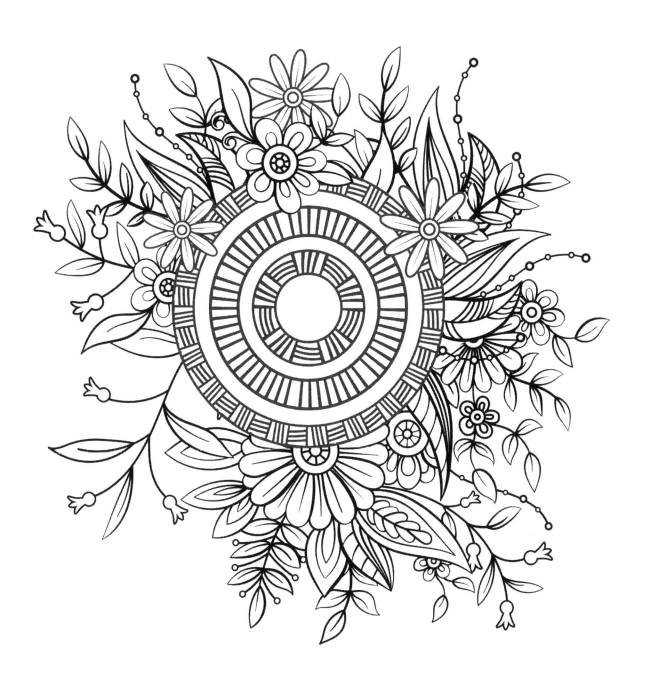

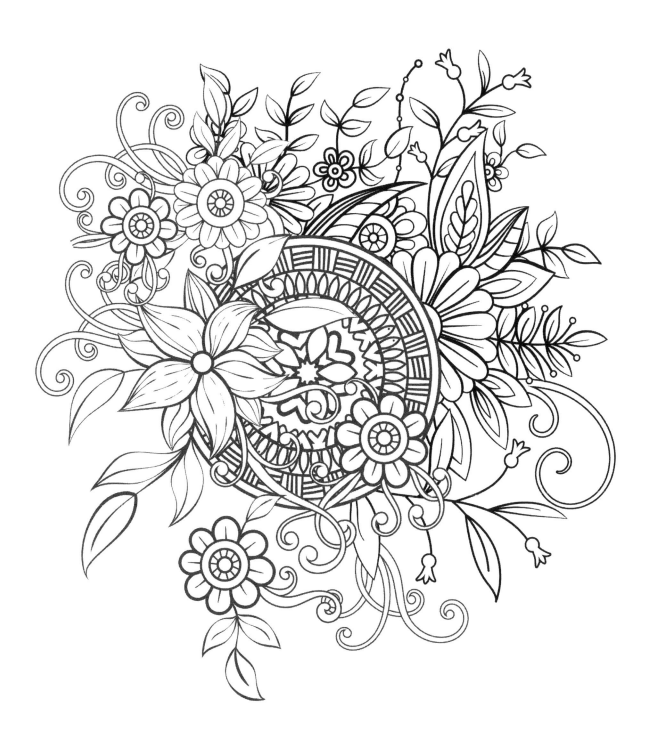

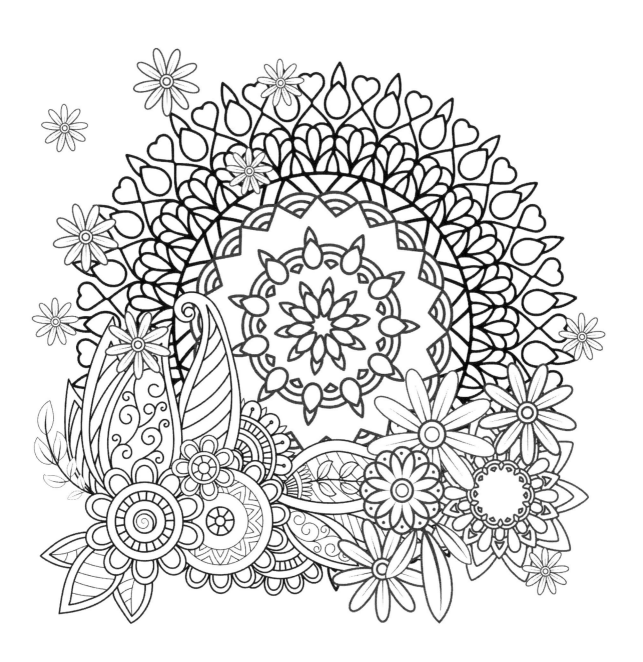

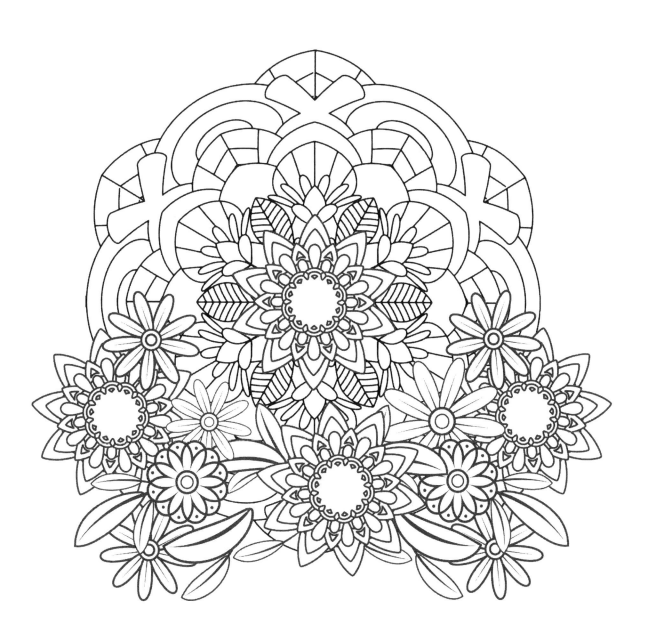

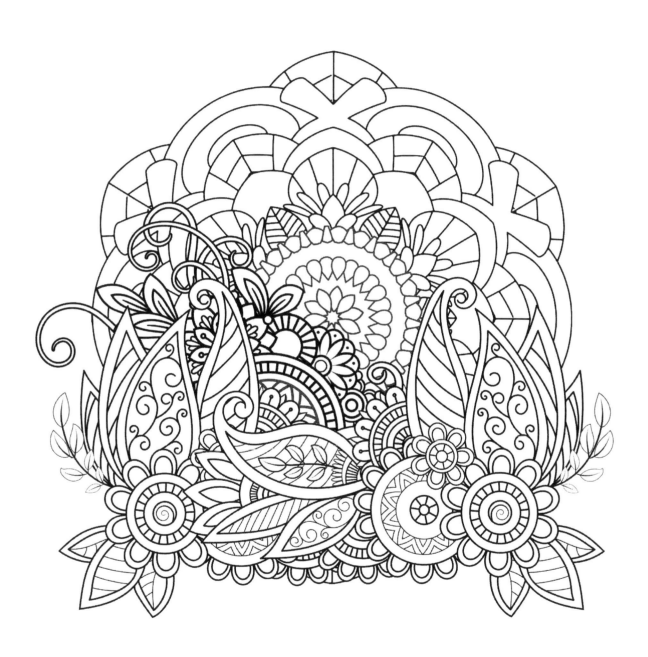

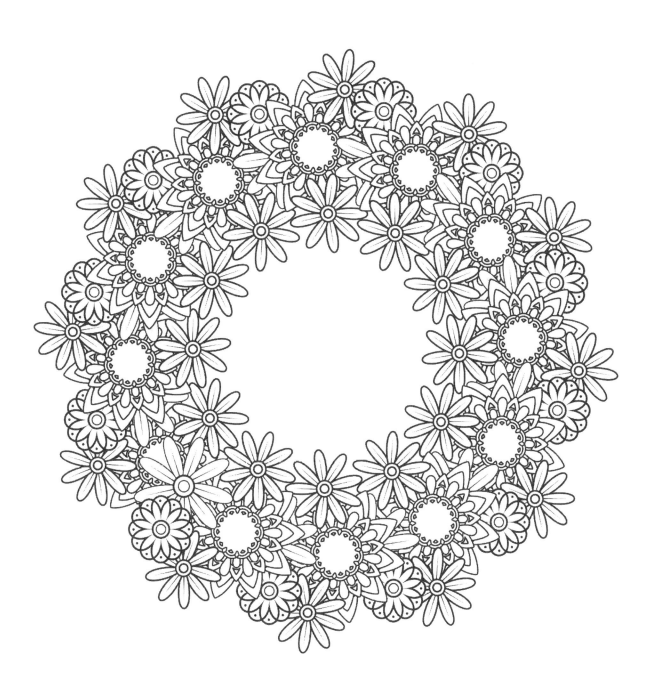

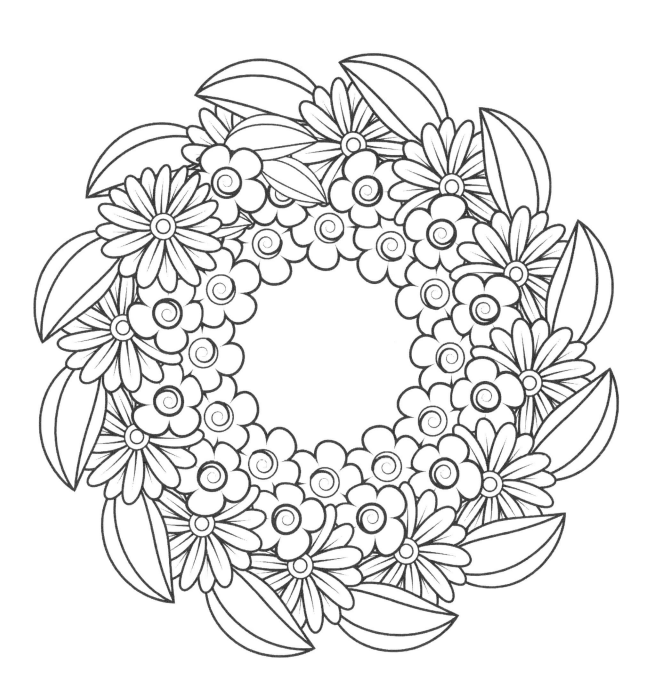

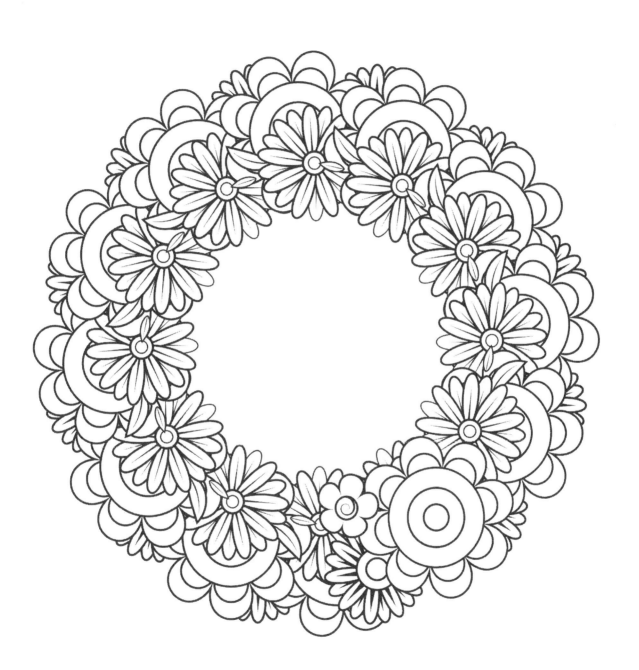

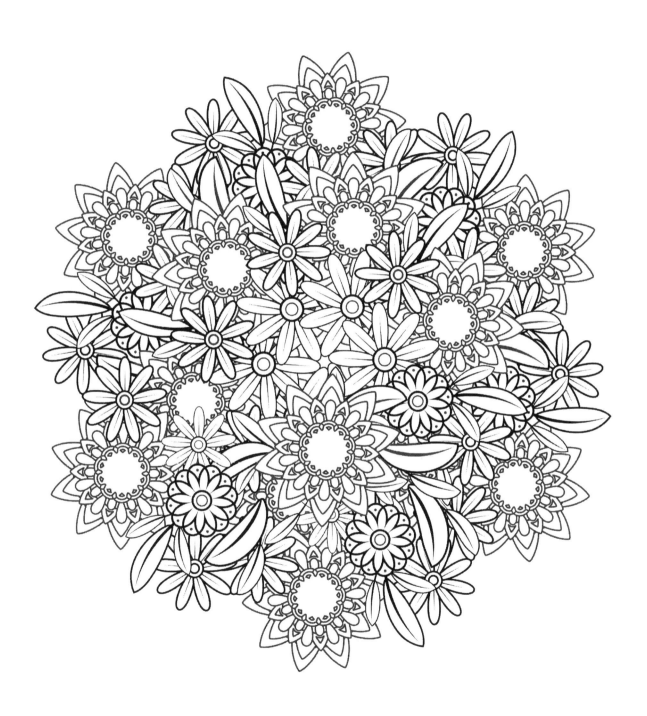

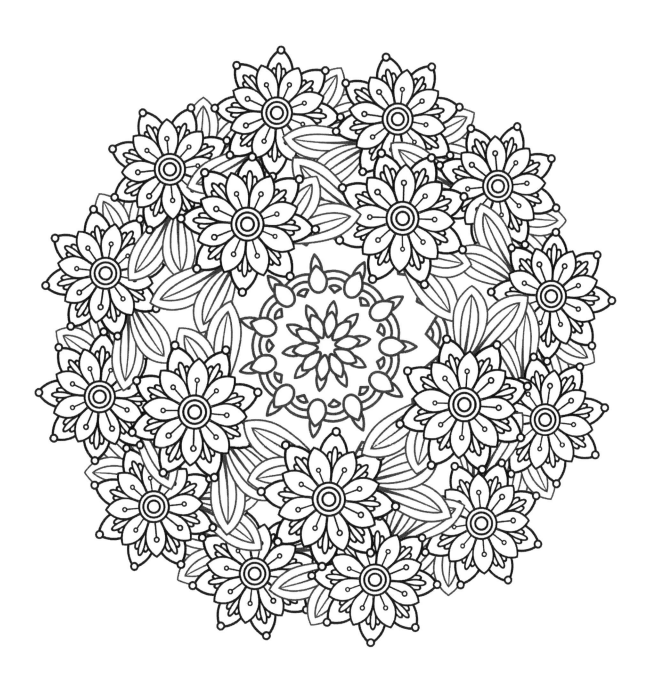

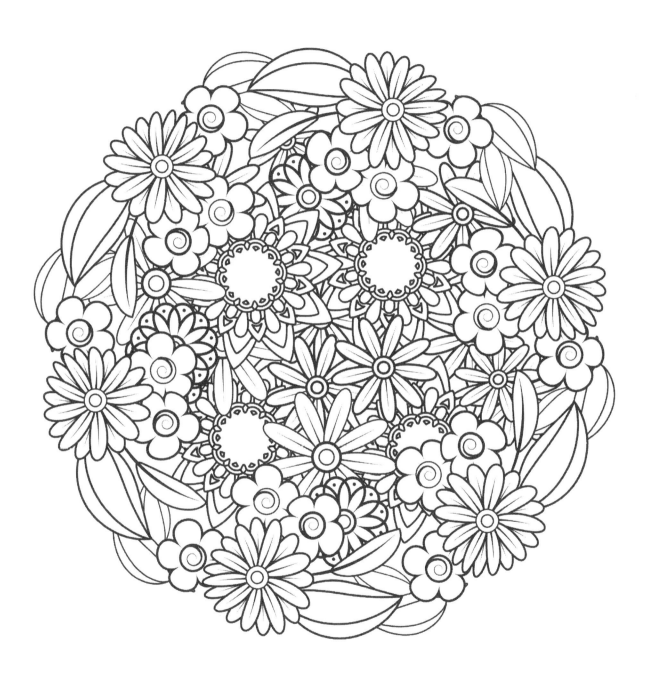

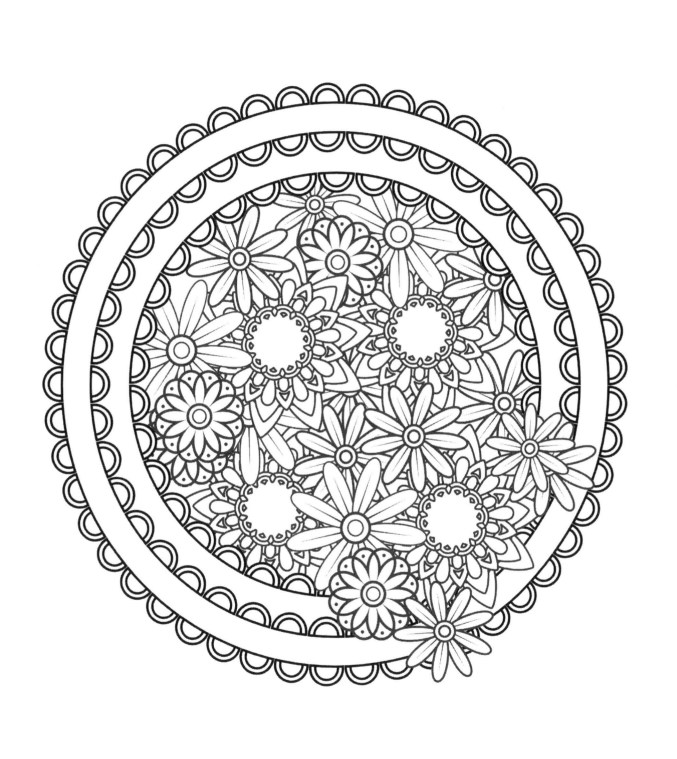

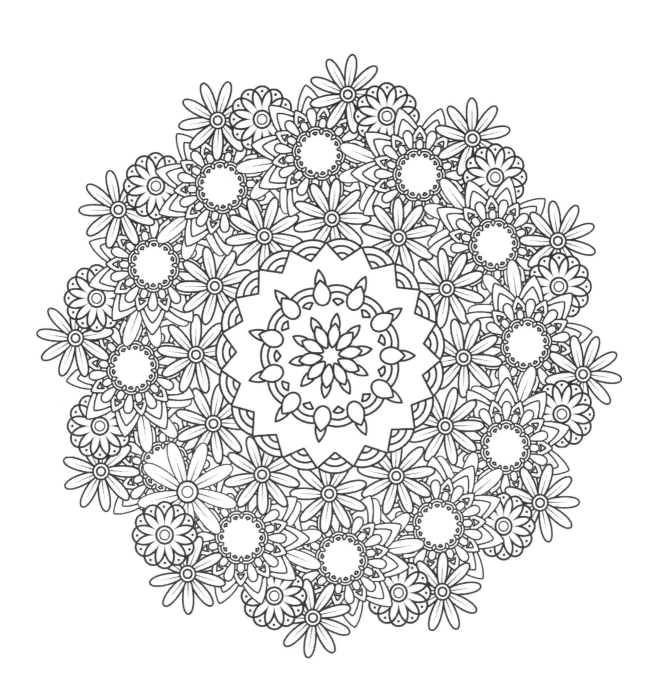

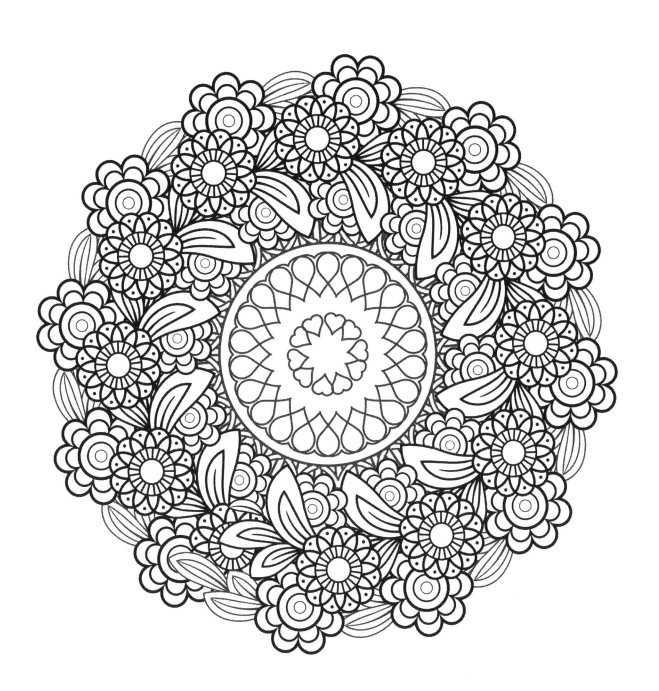

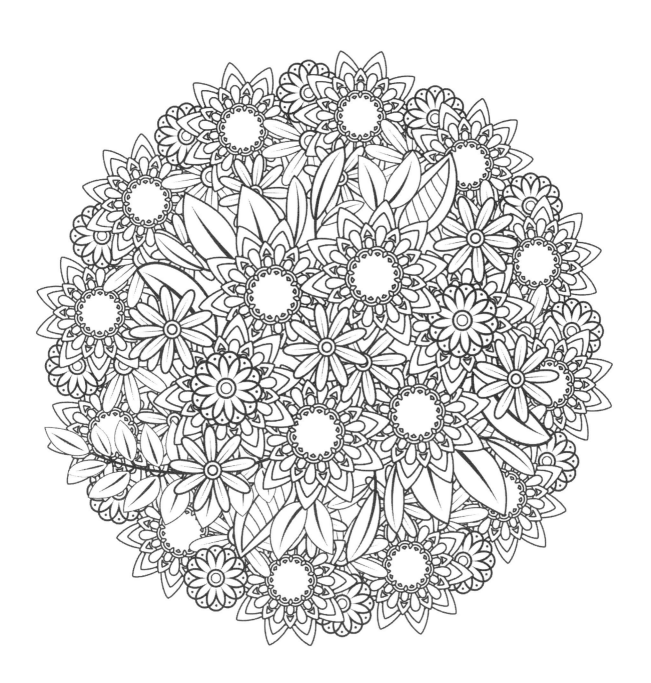

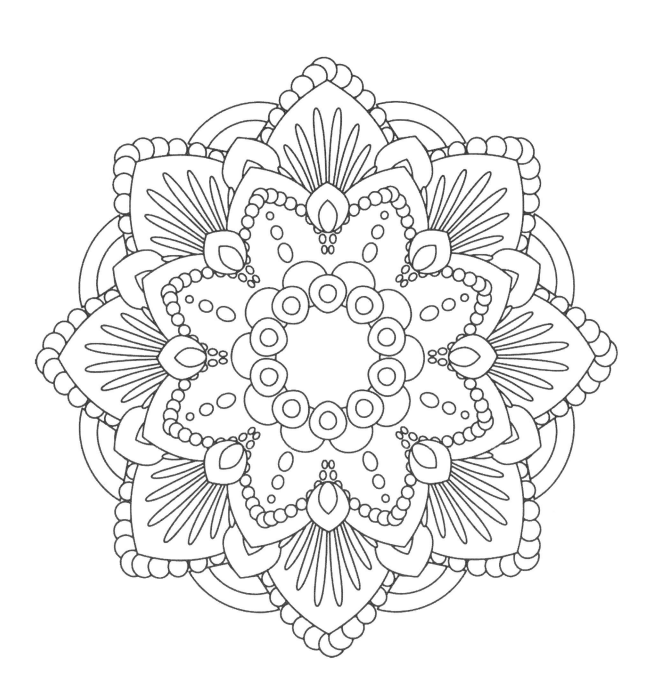

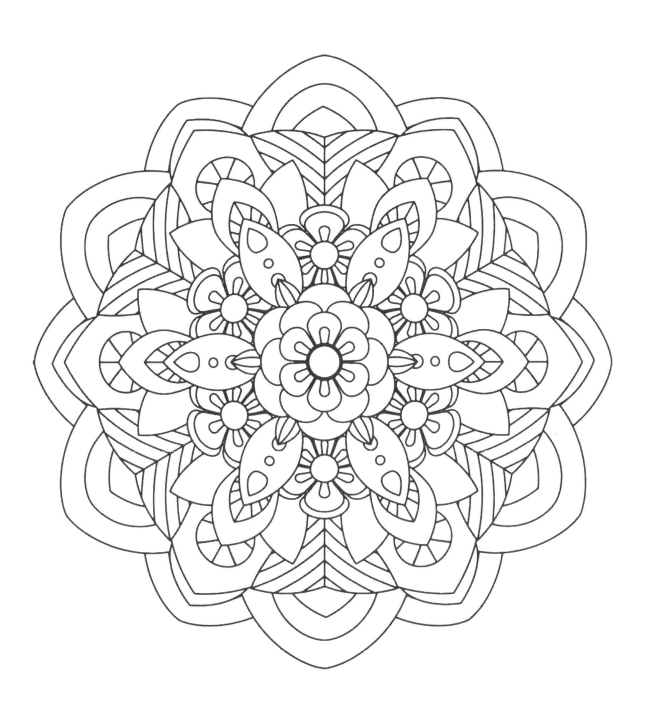

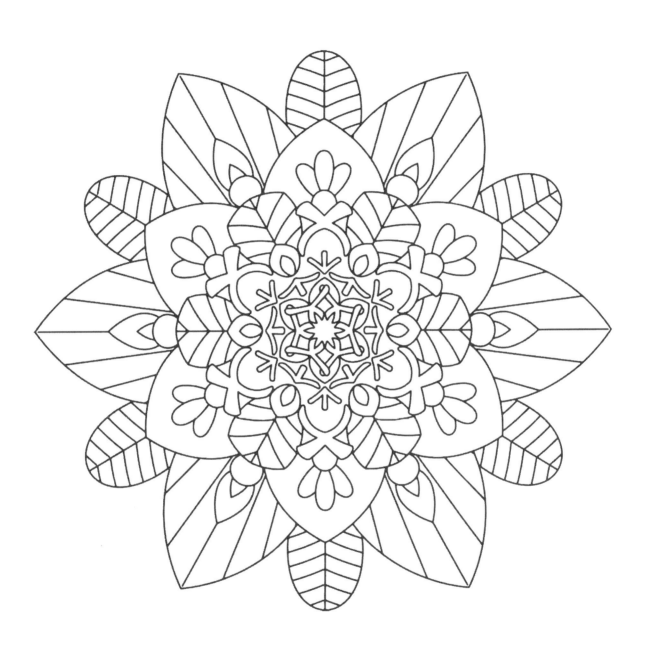

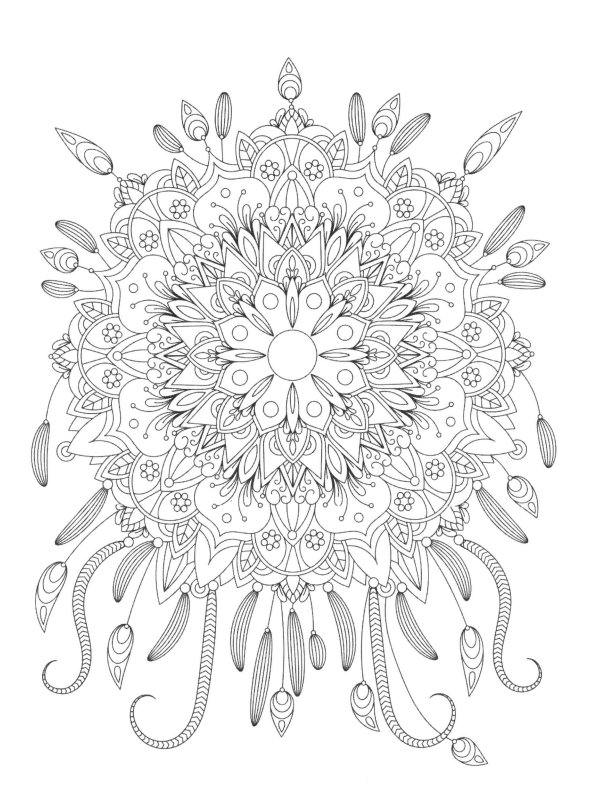

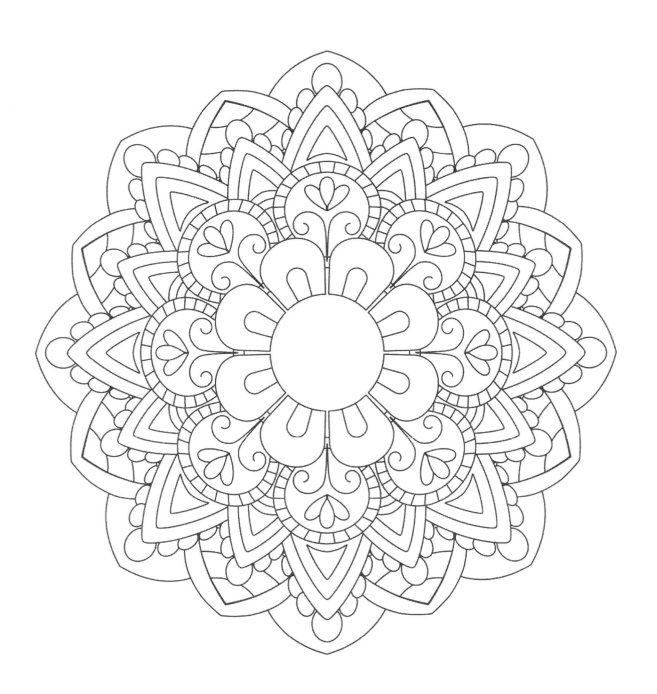

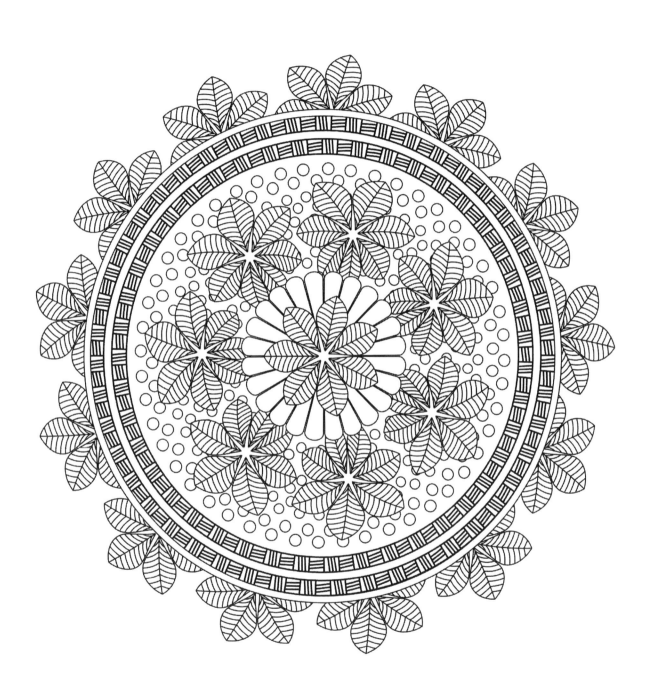

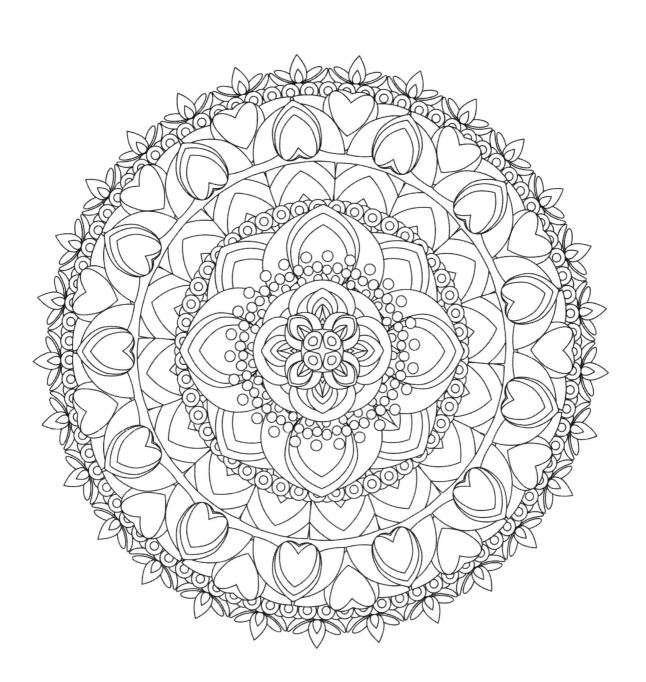

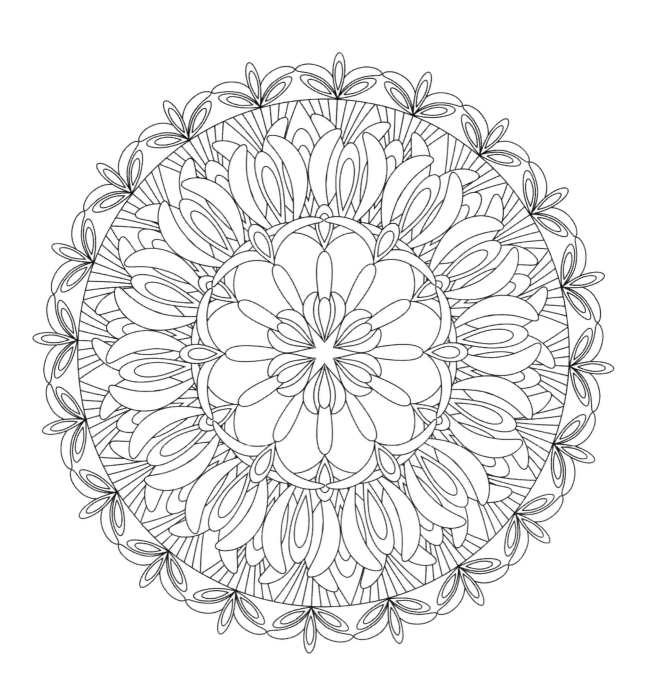

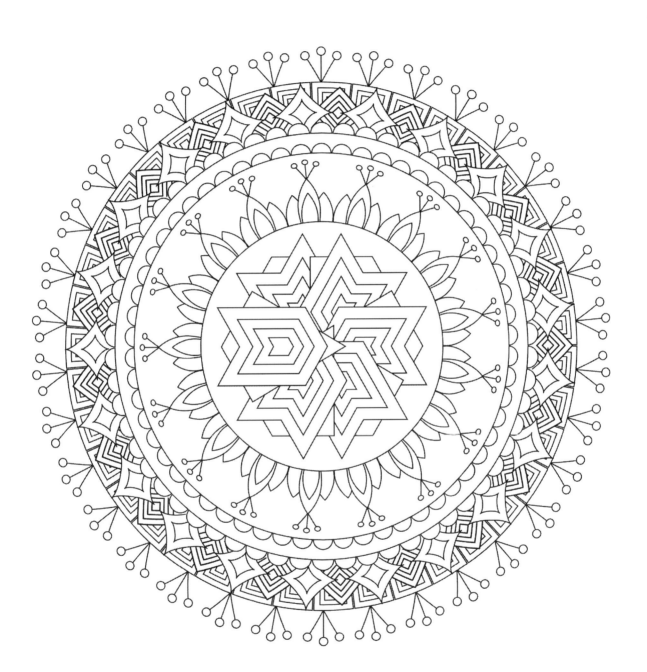

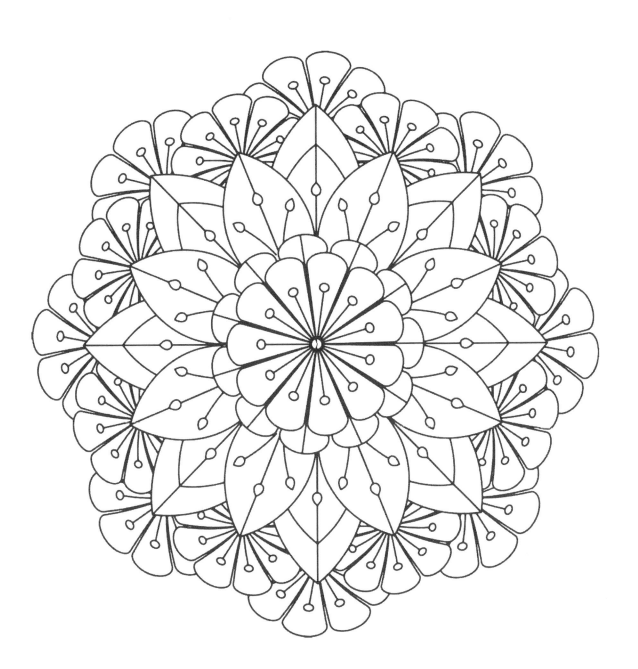

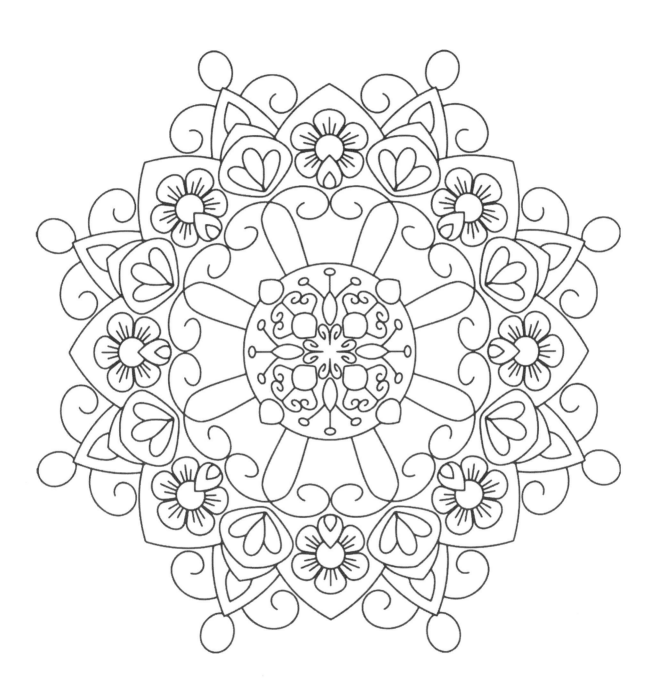

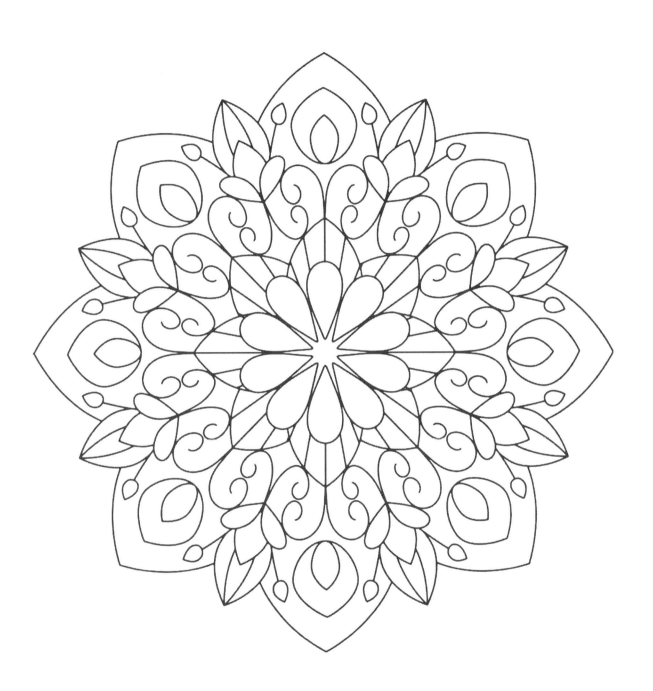

Made in the USA
Middletown, DE
09 February 2023

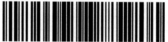

24325679R00038